PLACES AND
ELEGIES

First published in 1997 by **Salzburg University**.

SALZBURG STUDIES IN ENGLISH LITERATURE
POETIC DRAMA & POETIC THEORY
198

Edited by WOLFGANG GÖRTSCHACHER
and JAMES HOGG

ISBN 3-7052-0118-2

INSTITUT FÜR ANGLISTIK
UND AMERIKANISTIK
UNIVERSITÄT SALZBURG
A-5020 SALZBURG
AUSTRIA

Distributed by
DRAKE INTERNATIONAL SERVICES
Market House, Market Place,
DEDDINGTON,
OXFORD OX15 0SF
Tel: 01869 338240
Fax: 01869 338310

PLACES AND ELEGIES

poems and translations
1992 - 7

by

FRED BEAKE

UNIVERSITY OF SALZBURG

1997

For Marion

FOREWORD

The five years during which these poems were written has seemed a period dominated by great transitions, not least the approach of the year 2000. It has perhaps been the period in which the fact that Britain is no longer an empire, but a nation state, has struck home. Hence the need to readjust our horizon, hence the ode that concludes the original poems in this book, but also the frequent meditations on the passage of time. Hence "Elegies" in the title, in the sense of a laying to rest. Perhaps as a part of that, but separate, has been a need to come to terms with the being of places, and the past and future within them. But equally it has been a time of the passing of generations. Sorley Maclean, Brian Coffey and Brian Merrikin Hill, very different writers, but the three poets I most admired of my elders, have all died. However imperfectly, I would like to think that there is something in the poems in this book that is of them and for them.

These poems and translations were written in the period between the completion of *The Whiteness of Her Becoming* in early 1992 and the summer of 1997. The greater part of the book was, however, written in 1995-7. The book collects the work of 1992-7 except for the two long poems and group of short poems published in *Towards the West* (Salzburg 1995).

My thanks to numerous friends for their encouragement, notably in this time perhaps Marion Shoard, William and Patricia Oxley, Jon Corelis, Douglas Clark and Cath Finch. Jon and Cath both helped me somewhat beyond the call of duty with the Greek. Robert Palmer often gave help no one else could have done with computing and word processing, and more intangible matters. Dr James Hogg very kindly undertook the publication.

FRED BEAKE, Bath, August 18th 1997

ACKNOWLEDGEMENTS

Acumen published In July, The Light, A Beginning, Burnham Beeches and Ennismore Gardens, and two of the translations of Alcaeus.

Stand published the translation of Catullus 68 and Psychic.

The Poet's Voice published At Arbor Low, Stanzas at Dol y Cae and Mariner's Song, the translations from Callimachus, Antipater and Propertius, and the version of Samuel Johnson's poem to Skye.

The University of Salzburg Press published the two Theocritus versions in *Summoning the Sea*, an anthology of contemporary prose and poetry to mark the retirement of Dr James Hogg from academic teaching, edited by Wolfgang Görtschacher and Glyn Pursglove.

The World Treasury of Modern Poetry, edited by Katherine Washburn and John Major (World Book Club with W.W. Norton) is expected to include the versions of Samuel Johnson's poem to Skye and the Alcaeus poem to Castor and Polydeuces.

BOOKS BY THE SAME AUTHOR

POETRY

The Fisher Queen (Northern House 1988)

The Whiteness of Her Becoming (Salzburg 1992)

Towards the West (Salzburg 1995)

TRANSLATIONS

The Night of Loveless Nights by Robert Desnos (Xenia Press 1974)

The Peace by Aristophanes (University of Pensylvania Press 1998)

PROSE

The Imaginations of Mr Shelley (Salzburg 1993)

CONTENTS

Poems

Translations

POEMS

1 PLACES

I have always been interested in the essence of places, but it is really only in recent years that I have begun to look at scenes almost as a landscape artist might, recording particular moments and sights, and making poems from them. Equally in the doing of this new themes have tended to emerge, notably the decline of the British Empire in the last three pieces. Many of these poems are related to the love poems in section VI.

STANZAS AT DOL Y CAE

Easy for the trees to last,
    but some are rotten and list.
There must be fish in the lake;
    strange birds cacophonate.
Poets go unread and are poor;
    their kids get jobs and know more.
The wind of time pierces here,
    but till death I must utter.

Sense and sound outlast failure,
    woods and hills make soul laughter.
My head burns with deck-chair sun,
    old words find out their function.
I split logs for the next guests,
    know to Nature we are pests.

Yesterday had hidden shores,
    castled murmurs of cold wars,
Birds hopped, fence-post to post;
    unsheared sheep browsed among bones.
Cars mutter on nearby roads,
    jets scream the power of their loads.
The name of Cader is long here.
    Soon I must leave it to others.

Portray me with ancient beasts,
    I grow slight denied her breasts.

My son reaches for the top,
    I grow restless halfway up.

Note: Dol y Cae is an old farm house under Cader Idris

14

BURNHAM BEECHES

When the winds blow at Burnham Beeches
    and remove the gold leaves from the trees
there will still be that terrible quiet

and the sound of the fall of single leaves
    as loud and final as anything military
in the adjoining regions of our minds.

AT ARBOR LOW

The command to park had been in red, but where was
the notice to tell us the place of the stones?
There was clear indication of an electric fence

for the rest – great space, and green, and yet more green,
and worthy doggerel cattle, and a white dog
with black ears standing by rusted up machines.

The swift dipped down by the black barn roof, and I heard
like one listening from a great way off : 'Your son
is how old?' : 'Fourteen'. It was myself I heard.

'Doing 'O' Levels?' : 'Next year'. At last there's a sign :
TO CIRCLE. But there are mutters of Schoenberg, Webern
'A hard man' from the back seat. I had heard someone

– in the car – just a few minutes before.
And chamber opera. Now old trees come into sight.
One dead and broken and black called to mind Yorkshire

the dislike of males in colours in that pastel county
when I was young, a stranger, in that wild place
of the practical. But dandelions call me

and a tumulus up which a man pushes a
a baby buggy (hood up) to the very top,
the child laughing. From the top I can see trees

and horizons meeting, realize I was up
here with my grandparents, and have forgotten.
Did my father rush me up to the top?

Walk over towards the stone circle. Silence
except for birds, distant cars. Pause. Man and woman
– green, blue ; trousers, dress – join the stone liaison

of some in horned skins weaving dances to sun,
moon. Suddenly a rampart : pure blue vision.
Once over – daisies, a bee, cool wind and cold stones.

Children would play at sacrifice, propitiation.
I could really believe in a High One in the
caerulean waters we now think of as Space.

Were my mother, father here with me at the
horizon's turning point? Gran and Pa were I am sure
as now with bee, bird, breeze and noise of a camera.

IN WALES

Shrieking of jets preparing for War
    and muttering
of rock-shifting waterfalls

and two greens thigh to thigh
    one lit by the Sun
into a memory of aspiration

But in the grey air
    as if on slow lethal patrols
of World War One planes

the insect kind as there must have been
    when men harped of the hall of Cynddylan
whose lights were put out by the Saxon.

AT ILKLEY MOOR

The rock boulderous above
    from which some hebrew
might have made imprecation

to the wind, or thrown
    his flesh, that his spirit
might rise

against iniquity
    at the last edge of the dark
has on it some indistinct person

casting eyes at the vast
    horizon-reaching rotundities
of the Moor, which resembles

the great white deserts
    into which the seer went
in search of demons and the Truth

but we in front of lesser rocks
    make pictures
for the joy of making pictures

and are glad to go upon
    this place of people
and great visions

where the young encounter
    with the snow
and toboggans

while the grouse
  is vociferous
in the snow magic

and cannot (we assume)
  come to know us
unmakers of bird-kind

anymore than we can speak
  beyond the confines
of our tongue.

AT TEDDINGTON WEIR

Great crested grebes
   (where did anyone
see six before?)

but only their necks
   like periscopes
that divide

the shimmering
   of the river
in sun in February

by the antique blue
   suspension bridge
where lovers cross enarmed

and the tides
   of the sea
stop ...

Thames that was once the great conduit
   of the honor
and dishonor of this England ...

ENNISMORE GARDENS

The plane trees are so still
  on this February day of grey
when the great cold has finally sidled away.

Their large bulges are like the hides of those creatures
  that lurk as vengeful dinosaurs
in the minds of children brought up to suppression.

Most likely the trees grew before this enclave
  of once so modern colleges and museums
with names such as 'Imperial'

or 'Albert' or 'Victoria'
  now dirty with accusation and smog.
But these trees utter an image

of things beyond the temporal
  a great swaying between creatures in green
with two humans

touching as if truly there were no other human body
  and this place is all
and there is no carnivore

no greed for the possession of the human by the human.
  And young fierce men in Russian beards
building a church of strange stone

to maintain a reference
  against the arrogant race
that gave them shelter

but their names are gone under time
 with revolutions that never occurred.
And some of those ambiguous victorian English

chatting of far voyages and volcanoes
 and heresies about first beginnings
and questionable demands from the lower orders.

BY GREENWICH OBSERVATORY

Note in the distance the river.
But the forest of masts is felled,
and only the scream of waste industrial chimneys.

Nearer the gracious lines of the naval college
built by Charles of the many women,
Pepys of the single wife

who was never quite sufficient,
and left a navy as his descendants.
Here began that empire

that first broke Louis
who was a good ally
to ambiguous Charles

and then stretched across the seas
till in our time we were driven back.
But also gave to this home island

a tranquillity from war at the price of war
that made for unique evolutions, tolerations.
But the story is as much here

by this italianate brick house
with the names of the once famous
upon its façades

who charted Heaven and Time
that others might chart the seas ...
a man stooping over a dark image

on a table, that he might comprehend
the inner being of the lion sun
and not be undone

just as I look in the great flame that is you
and want to go on across whatever times or seas
there are in the time that is left to us.

II CHILDHOOD

We lived in an almost new house in Poynton in Cheshire. Opposite were some much older cottages in one of which lived my great friend Ruth, who I so missed when she went to school. Further up the road lived Vicky who to some extent took Ruth's place. We had a large garage (or it seemed so) but no car. Once at least my brother and I were allowed to play on its flat roof under the strict supervision of my father. There was also an air raid shelter which we were allowed to climb on, but not to go inside. From time to time the noisy jet fighters of that period shrieked overhead. There were some blackcurrant bushes by which I had a digging patch, and spent a great deal of my time. There was also some old wood, from which I constructed some rather unseaworthy boats. My grandparents lived at Leek. My great grandmother Lizzie Hughes lived with them. She was a great artist with a needle, and made me a wonderful series of children's toys, that were almost as real to me as the people round me. Bonzo the dog I think survives, but not any of the others. Visits to or from our Leek relatives were great events. I remember rushing along the lane with my brother in the hope of meeting the hired black car they came in, and being taken in the car and given Bonzo. Next door were two admirable school teachers, Miss Marsh and Miss Pritchard, who were very kind to us children. But I remember very distinctly the way the weather had almost a personality to me. It was no doubt the result of being out in the garden most of the day. It was a special and a happy time, and these poems tell something of it.

YOUTH

One day he will be truly a golden retriever
  but today is just a puppy
and a dull shade of grey.

He comes wuffing
  at the mowing of grass
but goes silent

and sits without command
  and watches
a long time for a small beast

as if partaking
  of some dark religious mystery.
So I remember I used to watch

when I was small whenever a workman
  came with paint or drill
to change the being of our house

And my Mother would grow uneasy
  in case it should lead
perhaps to some perversion

or was it simply the fear
  her child would get in the way
might even perhaps be hurt?

But at any age
  there is a glory in the first
sight and smell of something new and delightful.

EARLY EXCAVATIONS

'Are you digging to Australia' they used to say
   when I went out to dig and poke
  in the soil by the black currants
    close to Miss Marsh and Miss Pritchard's fence

And certainly there was a definite sense
   of reaching into regions that had to be reached
   and had no value in adult cash.
  It was the humid touch of the soil
   companionable like a mother's hands, and as cool.

But the sky above had a different being
  – sudden blues, gathering greys,
    rains that came, storms that failed,
   the sweet smelling brightness after wetness.
    This was like the moods of a mistress, or a virgin Queen.

EARLY PERVERSITIES

I cannot remember the face of Ruth
   from the timeless cottages over the road

who was bright with imperturbable joys
   and disappeared to school before Vicky did

and the visage of Vicky is wholly invisible
   – though she took the place of Ruth, for a while

But I remember the great thump of the borrowed
                                    [tricycle of Vicky
   when I rode full tilt at the garage door

THE TOYS THAT MY GREAT GRANDMOTHER GAVE ME

Any that would look for her in times past
    Know that she found love beside the fountain

And had a proud husband that lead paint bent down to death
    And children that War sidled round, but did not take.

She got her beer as the proceeds of a pension
    And had her brandy on prescription.

She guffawed at Lord Haw Haw, and claimed kinship with Brindley
    And retained a vestige of the Staffordshire tongue.

Sat up in bed in swordlike northern sun
    She gave me a duck with a red waistcoat

And that grey, suave dog Bonzo came at her behest
    In the hired black car of a grandparents' arrival

And there was an old unstable chair that was hers
    Long after her bodily departure

And she created the penguin I asked for on Christmas Eve:
    Though she had no pattern she knew the tradition

IV HISTORIES

I have always been fascinated by History. I have never forgotten my Leek grandfather reading J.R. Green's account of the Armada when I was very young in its sonorous Victorian prose. And all through my childhood and adolescence I read widely in History – Hawkins of Plymouth, The Age of Drake, *Runciman's* History of the Crusades, *Oesterley and Robinson's* History of Israel, *anything I could lay my hands on about the Dark Ages in Britain. However equally I loved Historical novels – Rosemary Sutcliff, C.S. Forester, Alfred Duggan especially. It was I suppose the counterpart to the fascination with Science Fantasy and Fiction that my son's generation has. I always intended to write historical novels when I grew older, and this who knows one day I may still do; but my interest in History has tended to surface in short ambiguous poems in the voice of a character who is not me. I stress this last because in a generation which seems determined to believe that all poetry is autobiographical this is usually regarded as strange. These poems arise out of the inner mind, as do most of the rest of my work, but they are not in my voice.*

AQUAE SULIS, A.D. 365

Below the hillside patterns of the vine
   In this chessboard town of holy springs
Most are concerned with pilgrimage and cleansing
   – even that slave greedily solicitous
to his aging master. But that one there
   has dark shadows on his face.
Does his owner weary of him now his bloom has gone
   or is it a question of a flagellation?
And you old woman with your tubby bum
   what message do you carry so cautiously?
What lucky youth or girl does your mistress send you for?
   She's married no doubt with skin like a fresh grape
and a girdle that will not need untieing.
   The marriage torch breeds conflagration
and duty and virtue remain in the parents' house.
   Some new Catullus will grow wise and sing her lies.
Or if not lust it must be religion:
   a missive to some pretty priest
on the subject of absolution:
   so much easier to be cleansed
by water than the rod.
   Our northern customs are so much milder.
But every chance its Zoroaster or that Christ
   whose followers raise tears of exultation
at an insurgent's crucifixion.
   But I have come from the northern hills
and the clammy stone of the Wall.
   I paused at my uncle the former proconsul's
but he gave me no answers.
   We talked of the smallness of our forces
and the rumors of coalitions
   the gatherings of fleets.

Now I go to pray
to the goddess of my fathers
the goddess of waters
knowing most of us are sinners
but that these people are my people.
For this I have come a very long way
and I shall return without hope.

TO RETURN STRANGER

To return stranger
into the outworld

by the fields of corn
and the hills

of sheep and tired slaves
and the litter of mines

past villas long built
to receive our Gods

and the native huts
whose gods keep their names

the remnants of the
intention of towns

is not the right road
but here among minds

that I know you loathe
– the ill-meant reports

the impossible and
always believed lies.

MARINER'S SONG

The albatross by some almighty engine
    passes the cloud ways with a sure direction.

We call, call against him
    and the grey, green slaughter waves.

We want treasure: intention
    we can tell women or sane men

but like the mad we grow used to a small room
    and engross in a dream.

THE EXECUTIONER

Wasn't inside as I remember,
But even if we were standing on a scaffold
In the middle of a lawn grey pillars
    And patterns of stone
Are not so far from what we felt
In those unforgiving times of Katherine's brat.

But whoever reigns they need someone to do the killing.

Jane Grey was so horribly calm
    While she was taking off her cloak
    And stepping out of her gown.
    But when she had taken off her bonnet
    And her neck was bare
    Strange shadows passed across her face.

I wanted it quickly over before she had time to feel her fear
    But she just stood there while the wind ruffled her petticoat
And I felt it was as if her soul had passed though she was still alive.

And then that fooling with the hankie
    Which almost unmanned me.
Just like a girl to choose a blindfold because it was pretty
    And not check it would go round her forehead.

And then when she was blindfold I sensed fear and outrage
    Like a child who would not take a whipping
    And thought of tying her down.
But she managed to kneel.

She cried to be put in the direction of the block
Did not seem to understand she had only to lower her hands to the boards
　　But old Sir Edward put his palm on her little white neck,
Her long back reached to the block, the wind stirred under her clothes,
And she was ready to be killed.

I brought the axe down and she just said 'glug'.
This was meant no doubt to be "God"'.
And then the stink of offal
And the showing of her frightened head.

I turned a girl like her off the cart
For taking a hankie like the one she treasured.
She had a back and bum so like that nine day Queen's
And for that I watched her dance with a certain pleasure.
I even tied her rope to make it last a little longer.

But if Jane Grey's death was quick and neat
Yet the approach must have been like weeks
At the end of a rope:
She must have been glad of her departure.

Elizabeth would not have taken off her gown with such a dreadful calm.
She would have sat on the boards and made a scene
And we would have ended with a new Queen
　　Or as bits on various spikes.
　　I do not think I could have saved my head and tied her down.

PSYCHIC

We are alone with the brown breaking cliff
and the fossils of earliest days.

In my dreams our love is still visible.
Could I make it real again

by leaping in the Earth Quaker's grey-green tides?
My love might well have done that when he was young

and Nothingness almost washed over him.
But I brought order to his dreams

and now it is I who observe
like a black squall upon the ocean of my mind

the chaos with potential for all beginnings
which soon must wreck what little's left.

But of this I cannot speak to him.
Is it to be divorce or a dying?

V CARTOONS

The poems in this section are very different to the last. They are intended as comedies on satirical themes. Any resemblance to real history is remote. The style is perhaps closer to that of a good newspaper cartoon, Low say. A reader would be well advised not to take too much literally. My politics are not those of the speaker in the True Ballad for example.

GOLIATH

Goliath after his technical knockout
    found himself short of employment
and had to send back his armour
    because he could not keep up with the payments.
And not wanting to be a burden on the state
    he got up at five in the morning
and scrubbed at the stone of a staircase. But
    he answered as one who had done the commanding
and they cast him out towards the Children of Judah,
    who knew that David had killed Goliath, so this man
must be an economic migrant,
    so they cast him out again
into the infinite desert. And it is rumored
    that he found his vision, and returned as a grain of sand.

ANDREA MACROBBERY

This next poem was lately discovered in the archive of the Bishop's Palace at Wells. It is by no means clear who the author of this strange document was. We note with surprise her interesting irregularity of meter and rhyme. We wonder if Elizabeth Barrett Browning had read her. Does more exist ...?

A Letter from Mistress Andrea MacRobbery, presently residing in Botany Bay, having narrowly escaped the Gallows under heinous Accusations, to her Sister Augusta, in England. Anno Domini 1799

Alas my Augusta, how dreadful the lays
    That you sent out so kindly, expecting my praise.
This thing about Tintern is straight out of Young,
    Except it is neither so wise nor so long.
We cut-throats and whores in a far distant land
    Expect our songs to be moral and our poets profound.
This silly young jackass, gone off for a walk
    Will be gone with the Season, just like a wheat stalk.
He makes not a mention – I remember it well –
    Of the Hell-like ironworks over the hill.
Still the Public is wise, and the thing cannot sell
    Except to the Young, who love every false thrill.
But to one such as me, who has been with great men,
    Known wealth and known wine, and the semblance of
                                                            [Passion,
And finding it gone like the mist from the sea
    Have turned from false lechery into brave robbery
Why the thing cannot do, the man is insane:
    He ne'er sat in Newgate awaiting his turn

– The cart out to Tyburn, and the long slow swing.
  What man is a man who has only his sister to sing!
But your affair with the Bishop sounds better and better.
  Know virtue then, and cease to be a whore!
Talk with him of mercy, and speak of your sister
  Misled by false men into utter disaster.
Let the King send a pardon right over the sea,
  And let me return from Botany Bay.
And if Mr Wordsworth should serve in your turn
  Well praise him most highly, and speak well of Tintern.

A HYMN TO POSEIDON

Steel cold fish clamorous by their silence stutter

Through the pig-snorting head of the great god Poseidon.

Above his grey bonce the almost invisible breasts of the air.

What down-swirl of sand troubles the aorta of the great one?

Only a memory of former gravels blocking the bladder

And giving Zeus an excuse to send Hephaestos

To do repairs that took in the scrotum of his filial foe.

And now Poseidon is a pig and pursuer of mariners

Who are intending only a little pillage and rapine

Of the sort the Market gives lawful occasion.

And every so often he gets angry and snorts on men

And various things are flattened in a most unseemly fashion.

Not a nice chap, Poseidon. And what his highness

Will make of these grey steel fish fucking with his head

That could well be the question of the decade, not to say
[the millennium.

POST MORTEM

Time flows in waves and I was at the trough

Not being Pope I was born in 1743.
Not being Coleridge or Wordsworth
I died in the city of Bath
   in Eighteen Hundred and Twelve

My early satires were found to be too conventional,
   My later lyrics tinged with obscurity.
Now in the Twentieth Century
   they have named a street after me.

But few I think have looked in the catalogue
   and sent the uneducated librarian
behind closed doors to finger dubiously
   tatty books, and produce a single volume
with the boards beginning to detach
   and the paper yellow
to find out what remains of a soul who wrote
   not as anyone's cur
but as the song lilted in the light.
   But the time was not right.

I was not like Clare,
   did not go conventionally mad,
nor was poor or of the oppressed class

nor like Manley Hopkins walked before my time.
   But the tune drove me on.

A single song they sometimes sing
    at scarcely attended recitals
graced Vauxhall once
    and made me a little money.
But my inheritance did not run out.

I lived soberly and quietly
    and was industrious for my Muse.
But the time was not right.

A TRUE BALLAD OF THE GLORIOUS
REVOLUTION OF 1938

Oh I joined the movement when I was just fifteen.
I was the truest Blackshirt that ever has been seen.
I was first driver to Oswald, and I kissed Diana's hand.
I tell you the Peace of Europe depended on that hand
For she us taught Adolph loves the peace, and Musso means no harm,
So we got old Winny locked away for causing false alarm,
And we sent stuttering George to Saint Helena, and
                                     [we called his brother back,
And we banned all un-English writers (especially William Blake),
And we treated old Stanley's constipation with the
                                     [marvellous castor oil.
But Neville was such a nice chap, and he understood his role,
And he flew over to Berlin, and joined us to that mighty club.
And we sent the Jews apacking in rusty sinking tubs.
Half of them drowned before the States, and half of them got over.
We had taken away their filthy lucre, but let them live to be poor.
Yet they spoke and muttered against us in the usual Zionist way.
They were all of course in the Great Conspiracy's pay.
The Americans in their usual manner got their knickers in a twist,
And Roosevelt sent his fleet against us after getting really pissed.
The Bismark led our fascist van, the Edward VIII our rear,
And we won a mighty victory by the Capes of Trafalgar.
Now Europe shall be united, and all drink beer in litres
In which we must toast gentle Adolph and Musso our saviors.
And soon the Bear shall succumb to our mighty attack,
And the mines of Siberia, and even Vladivostok
Will be given us by Adolph, who does not want it all,
But will reward the gallant ally who rallied to his call.

A PECULIAR GOINGS-ON

The sky was all grey
    so I went up on high
and asked of great Heaven
    what they had to say.

'Why! We needed new curtains
    in our front room:
this awful old blue
    made it a bit of a tomb.

We've got a new Creator
    who really is quite good.
He's told us to look at real things
    such as mud and shit and blood.

We've packed away old Nature
    (you only stood and stared),
we've gathered up the primroses
    and lady's smock you adored.

We're ironing out the crooked hills
    and bulldozing the snow-clad peaks,
and making every pebble
    a member of a clique.'

But as they spoke so proudly
    a little voice came by
and said 'I know I'm just the sun
    – and I really don't know why –

but I must make the ancient earth
   laugh and shout and dance.
I want the young men and the maidens
   to shriek in manic prance

and do the things their elders lack.'
   And the wild whimpering wind
said 'I've really got to go to bed,
   for I've sinned and sinned and sinned

and I've really got no energy
   to toss down the mighty tree,
and wear away the crag and hill
   down to the level of the hungry sea.'

And the sea said 'Anyway
   what is it to me?
If everything were all the same
   I'd want to do it differently.'

And suddenly the sky was blue,
   and red flags were flying,
and bright and dark were equally true.
   And there was a wild irregular singing.

VI BREVITIES

Poetically I grew up in the Sixties. Part of the atmosphere of the time was the search for the single image with large reverberations. Basho's haiku about the frog making outreaching ripples on a pond was widely quoted as the desired effect. I never in fact much liked the haiku, which seems an unnatural form to me in modern English. However the short poem of William Carlos Williams, Louis Zukofsky, H.D. and others has always meant a lot. To say a great deal within a short space has always seemed an admirable thing. It is after all one of the few ways by which a listener's attention can be held through a whole poem, though such brief poems can paradoxically be difficult for the reader on the page. In the Eighties I was briefly deeply interested in Philippe Jaccottet, who had I think similar concerns. However it was contact with the brief brilliant poems of the Greek Anthology that in the Nineties seemed to lead to this small flood of very brief poems, in a variety of styles, hopefully implying more than they say.

CHANSON

Under the wars of midnight we pursue cold stars
and our veins are virid like trees'

Only men of stone have joints calcined as ours

COLD LIGHT AWAKING

Cold light
awaking

soothes
the fevered

the young female
with the long neck

waves hands about
and moves her fingers

The older one sits intent
and interjects

The noise
is like a flowing of rain

on a shelter roof
broken

by the shutting
of a door

WE SURGE THE GREY SEAS

We surge the grey-green seas
  like the hopemender of man

In the distance a lateen
  and not merely a mizzen

But what of the end of the voyage
  – winter gales, and whales on the mountain?

A VENETIAN

Six good guns, paid for by a provident subscription, did not ensure
The protection of this Venetian under the sea shifts off South Devon.

A greater pirate than Man leapt on her from behind, and
                                                    [snapt her neck
And she was gone so quick the burghers of Teignmouth could
                                                    [not see their luck.

REGRET

Oh many
       many a year back
when I
      was barely in my force
on a sunnier day than this
            A. Ginsberg
tried to read
       from that empty green bandstand
of pyramidal roof
        and the traffic drowned him out

and now (I am told)
        he grows absent in the flesh

FOR BRENDA CORBOULD

There will be something like a strand beside the tides
and, on the sand, indentations of a passing.

Birds with orange beaks – and delicate feet –
will move aside to avoid those spots.

THE ECSTASY

The sky has that English dark
that lingers on the edge of grey

but through the crazed cathedral
a great oak

and in the former churchyard
a flame of poppies

and nowhere man, rat, or flea;
woman, fish, or mouse

but only one shape of size
and one much smaller

flitting through the ocean of Air

IMPROVISATION ON CHILDHOOD
THEMES

about the wind
        about the wind
by the bare tree
        on the frosted field
squeal of life against life

        hi ho
the river into middle reaches
        brown through
the manacled temples

        the child sings sings
as the pencil scribbles

        Into magenta of madness
first eyes strike
        light of drones
by the oak's green

        pain of words
    flames

outreach for silence
        among black rocks

the breeze sweet as unicorns

this is the place of no death!

INWARD

This girl – beneath her honey skin
    and bright skylarking face
hides what?

Does she slink within first tides?

A PRINCESS

Wherever it is she goes
  it is always a problem

to make an image out of water
  and the scarlet tresses of her gown

have more motion
  than the body of her youth.

MORNING AFTER

Crackle of grief...
                little girl beside her father
blue dress
            white collar
sucks thumb
                gesticulates
waves
            wellingtoned feet
high on a stool
                uncertain
of this adult height
                    even more
of the girl behind the bar

                            but for myself I am
in the grip of a grief

FOR SORLEY MACLEAN

My mind is on the face of an eagle
    attached to the head of an old man

that in my half waking seemed suddenly
    to leave off mortality

as it struggled on a moorside
    in face of a grey sky and the wind

assaulting without remorse or casualty
    any hint of human stability

and flashed like a reverse of lightning
    through the clouds of our vulnerability

so we are left
    with memory only

in which to fertilize
    whatever songs are to be made

COME SILENCIO

Come Silencio, son of mine
   hold hands up the hill of time
or fly like a rocket
   – pretend, pretend!

We will not go slowly as the trees
   or infinitely as mountains.
We had better scream a little, or dance.

Otherwise we will consider
the slow gestation of the star
and despair.

THE STYLIST

The easy stride of long well made legs
    against the stripes of a mini dress

A bag of string as if made for pegs
    held with arrogance across the shoulder

OUTSIDE THE NATIONAL PORTRAIT GALLERY

The faces of the street
  accumulate.
Mountains rise

in some, and nuclear
  towers, or woods
where the birds

are preserved for the hunter.
  Some look ostrich
at lovers

with evident other
  concerns, and some
are creeping

up like the wolf on the
  fold of the lamb.
Not as you

would see in a painting
  or a photograph,
not at all.

VI LOVE

These poems might I suppose be taken as telling a rather old fashioned story, of how a poet sensed love in the offing as it were for several years, and then experienced it, sometimes in ecstasy, sometimes rather less easily in reality.

POEMS AT MIDNIGHT

1

For the soup kitchen of her indifference
is an itch upon my skin

and the temperature of her magnitudes
cools wastrel want

for the magic is not yet beginning
though silence burns like a knife

and I cling to the hem of her dun jin
in a torrent of silence

and the emptiness of her nowhereness bites
and the heat of her tropics is broad

for the witchery of her mislove is sin
and the drift of her candle life

If I could attain into the fishes of her seas
she would set me to leap

2

For you are the stone of my beginning

and chattering across the forges of your roads

are the verbs of your surprise

for your mercy is a blood that litters

with the bleed of inner self

that the complex trap of kind

may not finally be an end

but all things be to moving

as presence is to mean

and chatterword of sparrows

cleanse and illume

and the heart of little foxes

be out of jungle born

3

You are the rush of sudden streams

that merely the jackthought knows

that catches at the flesh of lies

and finds sustenance in it

but you are whispered mutes

none ever worms to saying

and the spider of your weaving

goes not upon live dreams

4

I have glimpsed the bright living waters
　　upon planet unknown

I have called aloud for permission
　　to put down

The silence is prodigious
　　pain of stars

You are the one seeming
　　that matters to the end

but now I must sing to the utter end
　　which is beyond all death

Our tides shall be as the evening
　　going down into the night

our tides shall be as the evening
　　one slight grey in the ending light

IN DESPAIR AND EXULTATION

There is a sense of living breath

enough to make this man think of you at midnight
and know himself remade and yet hurt

that you must pass on like a dark wave
past the bow of a galley pursued without swerve

by the forces of righteous government
who do not notice the passing of this wave or that

but I notice it like one who has slipped overboard
drawn by the tuneful dark word of the water

but in this cold presence of alien fertility
must die unless you wash me from this sea

but out of the water I shall no longer be with you
unless I lie on the seashore and let you wash over me

A BEGINNING

Come
to me
in the hour

of your darkness
and the silence
of your meaning.

Do not
compete
with the

indifference
of the
great winds

or the lapping
of the waters
of Lethe.

Be as
a flower,
be flame!

TENDERNESS

Who to tenderness arises
  and breaks a selfish peace
risks hurricane and steepling wave

and sudden lightning thrust
  but sunny sudden after calm
and distant oak tops of unexpected land

IN A TIME OF ANGER

Oh you are now my own true love
  though winds wake greedy shadows

and the skulking of the weary sea
  portends a certain anger

and the gulls swoop disconcertedly
  and the spring-eyed sun is hid

but Love will ride these hungry seas
  that suck for its acolyte's bones

despite a failing bark
  pilot us to port

where – no magic balms to harm our joy
  or wholesome fruits to put aside

but harvest

SONG

The incandescence of our youth
is surely done
and never again will it return

but the blossom of our day
is not wholly done
and in time there will be fruition.

VII BATH POEMS

I have lived for a quarter of a century in Bath, but have always found it difficult to write about. In some moods I find it like living in a mausoleum, which is perhaps what that difficult poem Gabriel's Hounds is about, though it also brings in images from a couple of years in the early Seventies when I was in the wild North Yorkshire countryside near Whitby. Gabriel's Hounds indeed are supposed to move on the wings of the great winds of that area. The last poem seems to give some hope of a recovery of the Feminine, and either a move from this area, or a reconciliation to it.

10 A.M.

Another Spring, if slow

Greens become separate
and bright as a schoolgirl's face

At six there was sun
though my shoes were wet with yesterday's rain

The old supervisor
tried to listen, faking she is not deaf

I cleaned the classrooms
and Mike helped with the bright black rubbish bags

The light dances angular and bright
some goddess might be present in this light

But now the Sun has gone behind a cloud

GABRIEL'S HOUNDS

Between the hedge-lines and the cloud
  antiphony of howling

as if unbred hounds of old kin's doom
  had resumed their former flight

across our seas of computer and atom
  to break in the mounds of the head

and bring out the bones a thousand times removed
  a thousand generations nameless

casting on the wintering fields
  the chaos that leads to seed

but I who had seen sugared expectation
  turn to fungus on the fruit

ignored, put by the sign
  considered this merely a fox and a vixen

but now in the absence of love
  now the old patterns are in dissolution

and children strut their own webs
  and all over Europe men dream the old, bad dreams

I remember the Imagination and the Thing
  hoping to find absolution

for this city, this mausoleum of quiet ones
  whose music is of a single day and nothing.

A NEW SPRING

Dead leaves that escaped the winter
are jumping about in a brief escape
  from the pains of adult life,
but soon there must be dissolution

and the light of Her moves in angular
  but stately dances

We who were comfortable
  plan beginnings
regardless of their end

Shall we proceed to buy the equipment?

But we cannot stay here.
  It is as if we are trapped
between a wall of concrete
  and a man with a scythe
who in the absence of any grass
  will take any reaping available.

Come light of Her that was before man
  direct me in new dances.

VIII RHYMES

I wrote rhymed (or more usually half-rhymed) poems a good deal in the early 1970's, but then with very occasional exceptions the impulse seemed to die for nearly twenty years. For some reason however in 1995-6 it returned. This may have been connected with a good deal of exploring early Greek Lyric poetry, which does not rhyme, but is full of intriguing sounds, and moves with a force not on the whole given to modern free verse. Whatever the cause, the result was a group of poems which are full of the exploration of ideas, and in which the use of rhyme tends to lead from one idea to the next.

IN JULY

We are part of wave patterns like the sea
Or the wind moving among the stalks of the wheat
Or geese passing through winter in a bold V
Rousing rebellion in the adolescent

Or the tree that is finally dead and bare
Though it outlasted our great great grandfathers
And retired each winter as if to despair
At the summer's growth and the Spring singers

THE LIGHT

The road divides. Her heart-light flickers on.
Down which road? It is too uncertain.

A distant light, which might be just the moon
catches trees along the steep way down.

Another flickers in and out
as on some hidden lane a tractor thrusts its snout.

But where's the light for which I've searched
every hour without end for over thirty years?

I think I see it sometimes beyond a boulder
in the grey moor spaces of the inner mind.

I think I see it sometimes in the brittle day
but every time I approach it has gone away.

Perhaps if I follow some skywinding bird
I will find the true point on the card.

Perhaps I grasp where I should find,
or am I merely man who cannot see his end?

Surely her presence chimed once with mine,
but since that day I cannot find the tune.

Sin with age makes us all cynical
and our flesh grows brittle.

But still I reach for her, cannot escape
the distant beckoning light.

DAWN

Those that move within the night
  Meet their souls by the shadows of dark streams.
Great birds glide among shadows of metal.
  Morning's far and life teems.

Twin lights reign, fused together
  About the cubes of our defense.
The mind affixes ancient geometries
  To things that were conceived by Science.

IN THE GARDEN
OF AN ANCIENT FARM

They lie on the autumn lawn
　　grey feathers of some one time being.
The under-white　is interesting.

And now the children of this house
　　grow to adult shapes
and seek the customary escapes

between the thighs of unsuitable lovers
　　whose blood bold Nature insists
will ensure the breed of their kin persists

into futures less certain than bird or leaf's.
　　Strange indeed the temporal shadows
that loom over the children of this land.

FOR THE GHOST OF
PERCY BYSSHE SHELLEY

I do not know how to look at these followers
  Of official lines, who can't make a verse
Unless it please the god on high's nostrils
  And moves in rhythmless lifeless meters

Or else look to the common crowd and prance on
  Some stage in mockery of their own art,
Or summon mock angers off the TV screen
  And speak correctly when they ought to fart.

But those that oppose the darkness of this
  Creep in cold ghettos where the words have no sense,
Or speak subdued, their verbs without force.

Till the new tongue utters, till the rivers
  Underground since the time of Bysshe Shelley
Emerge, English verse shall be under shadows.

TO FOLLOW THE WATER

In-arrowing damp log walls that never meet.
Might be of some hall, some Grendal's cupboard.
It is some vague fretwork of this middle life time.

I am surrounded by help wasters – good maids –
but like little Bo Peep they have lost their sheep
and their inclination is not to be brave.

Oh for hill air and some patch of gathering blue sky.
But those days are gone – and its utilitarians
(romantics all) making the best of it dolefully.

Perhaps it is as once I could not begin
to find a way up the black sheer crag rocks
and walked round to the other side with no intention

except to go, and found the way unlocked
and an easy ascent to a view of flowing green,
and still blue sky, and murmuring dissent

such as is not approved of by those who want
a pretty scene to put up on the wall
till the next divorce, and are always kempt ...

budding trees and a white bridge over
pebbles that the water's passion has washed clean.
Time it must be to follow the water.

IX

ODE FOR AN ENGLISH MILLENNIUM

ODE FOR AN ENGLISH MILLENNIUM

The patient tide of whose heart
   is the murmur of our sea
moves inutterably in the stark
   crystal of eternity

and shifts the fallible iniquity
   into a bad-eyed dream
for the posterity that shall be
   different from all we've known or been.

The essence of our material pride
   waxed wild in Hereward
after the arrow brushed the King's helmet aside
   and stone of old churches was overturned.

The poet sang beauty in a London dawn
   though love-hurt himself, and knowing corruption gnawed
the vital organs of a humorous nation.
   I stand as it were on an onanous shore

seared by the sensible doing of little things
   the return of the poor
the insidious niceness of commercial wrong
   blank indifference to past or future.

Send us some inner outlaw
   send us some dream of love
not little things through a magic door
   nor Eros as brother to War

but a mental wood where men may find
    a place of faith against the dark
sure enough to roar with the boughs in a high wind
    and forget the thorny wastes and the sun burning

and when Spring comes with its tide of despair
    and there are seeds impossibly to rear
let us speak of Alfred, broken in war,
    or of a young princess for whom the block was near.

Note: 'the young princess' is Elizabeth I.

TRANSLATIONS

ON THE TRANSLATION OF GREEK AND LATIN

There will be those who will notice the translations in this book and pass on with a sneer, muttering about things from another world which are of no relevance to this time. And there will be those who will regard them with a veneration that is probably a severe handicap to any real engagement.

What I would personally ask from a reader of a translation of mine is a willingness to judge it as a contemporary poem, and one which meant almost as much to its author as the originals that accompany it. 'An odd idea' you will no doubt observe. However, it is how much of European Poetry has operated for three thousand years. When Horace and Catullus came to write they often started with a Greek original. Indeed one recent American feminist scholar sneers at Catullus because he "only" translated Sappho. This is half true. Indeed there are Catullus pieces (as Germaine Greer has recently pointed out) that are the best clue to a missing or incomplete Sappho original. However one has then to say that Catullus makes a superb job of the transcription, and makes it so much his own that it scarcely matters. It is more like a folksinger adapting an old burden to his present situation than translation, let alone plagiarism.

Then there is Virgil taking the ground plan of the *Odyssey*, treating it like a jazz improviser does a set of chords, and producing the *Aeneid*, or indeed Propertius writing brilliantly about a difficult love affair in Ancient Rome, and dovetailing it in with matter from the learned Greek Elegiacs of Callimachus.

But it was not only the Ancients. There is Campion in the Sixteenth Century taking the tune of Catullus's superb 'Vivamus mea Lesbia atque amemus' and varying it enough to make it his own. There is Pope writing brilliantly about his own age, while giving us the most acute versions of Horace. There is Samuel Johnson taking Juvenal as the ground base for his own deep passionate arguments with his own age. Shelley took Aeschylus as the starting point for *Prometheus Unbound*, and Greek in general stimulated both his melody and his sedition.

Hopkins was an outstanding Greek scholar, and owed something at least of his theories, and perhaps even more of his sound to an awareness of the irregularity of the Greek chorus with its quasi free verse. And over the channel Rimbaud wrote good Latin verse when a schoolboy, Baudelaire has at least some awareness of the elegiac poets, and a number of poets at the turn of the century seem to have been affected by the complex structures and sonorous irregular melodies of Pindar.

In our own century the best has often had classical relationships, whether it is Edward Thomas' slightly dolorous, rather Horatian sound, Ivor Gurney possibly at least taking some of his odd word order from schoolboy Latin and Greek as well as Hopkins, or Bunting producing the most real imitations of Horace's formal yet colloquial odes.

However the great influence was on the Americans. Pound of course developed his short poem at least as much from the Greek epigram as the Haiku, and while they are not identical the disunified unions that are his *Cantos* bear some relationship to the thematic, often disjointed forms of Propertius, Juvenal and perhaps ultimately Callimachus. H.D. (still perhaps the most underrated poet of the century) learnt most of her Greek after she left school, and took from it both a context for her personae, and a style of melody, which, though not identical to the old forms had something of their feel. Zukofsky thought it worth his while to transcribe the whole of Catullus into a strange post Joycean idiom, and also to make one superb straight version. Again his melody, though different to the Classics, bears their imprint. Williams, though not a classical scholar, was always interested in the Classics, and something of their lyric forms seems reflected in his very different unrhymed structures. In his old age, when otherwise writing very directly about contemporary America he thought it worth while to get Greek scholars to read Sappho and Theocritus aloud to him in the original, and make versions which compare very favorably with their academic rivals. His pupil Ginsberg thought it worthwhile not very long before the composition of *Howl* and *Kaddish* to examine the Greek metrical theories in some detail. Olson rather improbably imports Greek words into Gloucester, Massachusetts and its rough fishermen. One could indeed claim that nearly all the great American poetry of the first half of this century is in direct line of descent from the Greek poets.

So how is the teaching of Latin and Greek out of date, or irrelevant? Only it seems to me in the minds of very second rate educators, who lack the courage to engage the best; or of poets who have lost faith in their art as a long term thing, but see it only as a narcotic for immediate woes. "What's the use of it?" said some utilitarian politician to Faraday of his obscure experiments in electricity. "I don't know, but you'll tax it" was the reply. So much of our age is beset by the same problem of immediate worth.

Yet what have I got out of my long engagement with Latin and Greek?

Firstly when I was young a sense of something new. This came two ways. There was the sense that here was a new tune, a way of arranging syllables, that was manifestly different from either free verse (of which, at that stage, I think I knew perhaps one poem each by Eliot, Lawrence and Whitman) or the traditional rhymed meters, which (though I love them) have never come easily to me as a poet. Then there was the sheer wizardry of the sounds and feelings I encountered. To take just one example I have never forgotten the sound of Virgil's bees when I did the fourth book of the *Georgics* at 'A' Level. Did Sylvia Plath know that sound too? Her bee poems are the only ones like it.

Later on (and not incidentally at school, but in books I found for myself, much as H.D. must have done) there was the melody of Horace, with his ability to say much briefly, with his willingness to be passionate one minute, and ironic the next. Also Catullus with his deep passion whether in love song, or satirical epigram. They made me ponder a lot on the order of words in English. Horace seemed susceptible to being translated into a colloquial English, almost word for word with the original, provided the grammar was sidestepped. Catullus and Horace interacted with my early discovery of Williams, Pound, Zukofsky and Bunting. I doubt if either would have meant so much without the other.

Later, after I gave up Latin after my first year at University, I rather perversely discovered Propertius, Tibullus and (to some degree) Juvenal, and also pushed further in to Horace. I was struck by the disjunction of the Juvenal *Satires* and the Propertius *Elegies*. While not as extreme as the *Cantos* or *Wasteland* you could see where Pound , Eliot and Bunting had come from. Pound almost did not need to cut up Propertius, for Propertius is already very modern!

In the Seventies much of my time was taken up with strategies for formal verse not in the main English tradition. I took from Latin a tendency to a final foot of two syllables. I experimented in the dark punk England of 1976 (such a contrast to a decade before!) with making my own paraphrase of Juvenal's *Vanity of Human Wishes*. I wanted a rough equivalent to his hexameter, and found it by taking a fourteen syllable line and dividing it into four feet of three syllables and one of two, with underlying pattern vv–. To get the desired melancholy I also used part rhymes between each couplet. This led a couple of years later to a straight version of Tibullus 1.X (which many think my best translation) and uses an unrhymed couplet of

97

3,3,3,2; 3,3,3 again with a predominant vv– pattern. This form with increasing variations was important to a lot of my poetry of the Seventies and Eighties.

In the late Eighties and early Nineties I struggled into competence in Greek with the admirably patient help of Cath Finch (later Head of Classics at King Edward's, Bath). By 1993 I was reading and translating a good deal of the poetry. I found the language (while precise) more relaxed than Latin or the American Modernists, and this I think has left a deep impact on my recent writing. I was also bewitched (as perhaps not since I encountered Virgil, Horace and Catullus) by the sound. Early Greek particularly, whether Homer, Sappho, Alcaeus, or the lesser known writers, such as Tyrtaeus or Minmermus or Theogonis, fascinates me. I hope – however remotely – that some of the melody has touched the poems in this book; but no doubt this is the arrogance of Horace when he talked of having brought the Greek Metres into Latin, though in so doing he remade them into something new.

I TWO POETS FROM IONIA

ALCAEUS AND SAPPHO

These poets wrote in a dialect of which little else has survived. Both were writing in a sophisticated yet popular form. Alcaeus is frequently (but by no means always) political, and his language is powerful and compressed. Sappho had a gift for simple lines that resonate. Her expression is direct, and yet (rather like Mozart) there is a depth under the simplicity. The sound of these pieces is wonderful (rather like Campion) in spite of (or perhaps because of) their being written to be sung.

ALCAEUS

TO CASTOR AND POLYDEUCES

Come! Put by Pelop's isle
Zeus' and Leda's hero sons
Castor and Polydeuces
Come!

Over the earth's breadth and the width
of the Sea come swiftly on strange horses.
You can take away death from these men
great cold threats.

Quick! Up the mast of the well-built ship
bright from afar. Quick! Up the rigging.
In the pain of night bring light
to the dark ship.

ABOUT HELEN

So written : mind-pain for wrong. So it came
to Priam and his sons alike, Helen.
Because of your fault Zeus burned down
Troy's holiness.

Not such did Peleus, not such a female,
having called the blest to a mating,
lead out from the Halls of Nereus,
but a tender young woman

to the homestead of Chiron ; and loosed her lust
with her girdle. And they made love
he and that loveliest Nereid.
And in a year

a son became – greatest half-god,
blest in goldenness, driver of fillies.
But through Helen a city vanished
and all the Phrygians.

TO MELANIPPUS

Get drunk with me Melanippus. Why imagine
    that after the great ford of eddying Acheron

is crossed there is the holy dawn and the sun
    to look back on? Come on! No big plan!

Sisyphus someone's said – Wind King's son
    and best of men – thought to order Death

but though he was canny in his head and made it back
    over the eddies of Acheron

the Son of King Cronus had a job for him
    under the soil of Earth. Come on! No expectations!

We are young and now if ever happy:
    We can endure whatever Heaven sends, however soon.

Under a city roof let us share a lyre
    to the rising of the North Wind.

SAPPHO

TO ANACTORIA

Cavalry in array, or infantry
or galleys some call the loveliest thing
on the soil of earth, but to me it's the love
of human for human.

No problem at all for anyone
with any sense. Helen whose grace
exceeded all human left
her perfect man

made off, and sailed to Troy
and as to her child or loving parents
she gave them no thought but love led her
quite off course

...which brings Anactoria's name to me
who is not here.

I prefer her loved walk
and bright and glancing face before
all the chariots of Lydia, or the footbattlers
with their weaponry.

TWO FRAGMENTS

1.

At the top of the highest branch
    there is a red sweet apple.
The pickers cannot have noticed it
    – or rather noticed and could not reach.

2.

Hesper returns what Dawn scattered
    – sheep, goat, and child.

TO HER LOVE

I think he is Heaven's equal
who gets to sit by you
and feel the sweet overtones
of your voice

and your soft laughter, that make
my heart pound in my chest.
When I look at you, however briefly,
there is no speech

in me, my tongue's snapped off
and flame creeps through my flesh.
There is no seeing in my eyes, or hearing
in my ears,

sweat pours from me, I am all
trembling, and greener than grass blades,
and I feel I am only a short
distance from death.

II BREVITIES

CALLIMACHUS, ANTIPATER OF SIDON, SOLON OF ATHENS (?)

There are a lot of short poems in Greek. Their terse ease is perhaps the counterpart of the long poems and plays. Here are a few examples. The Solon may indeed be by that statesman, but if so would have had something of other folk poems on similar themes.

CALLIMACHUS

FOR HERACLITUS OF
HALICARNASSUS, POET

He told me Heraclitus of your end.
    Tears came to my eyes. I thought of
how often we sank the Sun with chatter.
    But you my Halicarnassian
are somewhere ashes and History.
    But Death that lays hands on
all mortal cannot delete
    the life of your songs.

ANTIPATER OF SIDON

FOR DIOGENES,
SON OF CALLIGENES OF OLYNTHUS

Know he cut to Atlas Straits
    and tried the fertile waves of Crete
and all the navigation of dark waters

But he met death in harbor
    slipping off the prow at night
throwing up too much to eat

So little water took him
    who had essayed
the greatest seas.

TO ORPHEUS

Never again Orpheus may you lead tree spirits magic-bound
   or rocks, or the autonomous flocks of the beasts.
Never lull the gnaw of winds, hail, snows'
   gatherings, or sea's clashing.
You are dead, and the daughters of music
   mourn you, not least your Mother, Calliope.
Why cry out at son's dying, when the force
   of Gods cannot keep their own out of Hades?

ANON possibly SOLON OF ATHENS

THE WISDOM OF SOLON

He is the equal in income
of the man who has masses of gold
silver and acres of wheat bearing land
and loads of horses and mules

who is comfortable
in his stomach
loins and feet
which is all a man needs

for however much wealth you have
in this world
no-one has gone with it
into Hades

and no bribe evades Death
or the burdens of ill health
or the grey coming
of Age

III THREE ROMAN POETS

CATULLUS, PROPERTIUS, HORACE

To come to the Roman Poets after the Greek is to enter a tradition with much less of a history. Greek poetry started with Homer, or quite likely earlier, and always had a strong folk element. Roman Poetry is essentially the creation of a few geniuses in the two centuries before and after Christ. It borrowed frequently and unashamedly from the Greeks, but it transformed what it touched into something highly individual, more earthy, and on the whole less folky. There is more wit, and more melancholy.

CATULLUS

POEM 68

NOTE

The poem turns on a simple parallel. The mythical Laodamia lost her husband to the Trojan War after only one day of marriage; Catullus has only managed one day alone with his married girl-friend. Laodamia's husband was the first Greek to die at Troy. Hence the oracle he would not be gone long.

So you write to me now, luck gone and chances sour
    a letter assembled in tears.
Shipwrecked and hurled in the white storm water
    it is I who must raise you from Death's door you say
who Venus the holy does not allow calm sleep
    in the desert isle of your womanless bed
who the age-old gentle classics of poetry
    do not soothe in the sleepless night.
It is good that you look on me as your friend
    and demand the modern version of love.
But as you know I have my own troubles.
    Please do not regard my refusal as rude.
You will have to put up with this from a man Fate's waves lash.
    I have no better at this time!
When the garb of purity was given to me
    and my life was in the spring of it's flowering
I overindulged in sex. Our Goddess is Love
    and she mingles delight and despair.
But then my Brother died, and I turned away
    from all that. Oh my brother, taken from me!
Your dying dissolved my living, brother.
    In your going was the end of a family.
Any delight in life has left me
    for your presence gave it light.

114

When he was gone I put out of my mind
    love and all mental pursuits.
And you write to me that my way of life at Verona
    is wrong, and those who have any sense
find warmth for the cold limbs of an empty bed.
    But this is necessary mourning, not melancholia.
So now you know the grief that weighs me down.
    There are no poems, I am silent.
And I am afraid I have no good books to send.
    My home is at Rome
where I plucked the flowers of my youth
    and of many books I have one here.
This is how it is, and you must not think me hostile
    or in any way lacking in generosity
because all that you ask is beyond what I can do.
    I would if it were within my means.
But Muses, despite this I cannot stay quiet
    about all the things in which Allius has assisted me.
If I do not speak the oblivious centuries
    will cover his love with a dark that has no light.
I tell you this for you to tell it to many
    and they to inform generations.
Let Death be the beginning of his fame.
    Do not let the sharp needle of the spider conceal his tomb!
Now you know all the problems that the trickeries
    of Amathusia brought down on me.
She scorched me till I was hot as the rocks of Mount Etna
    or the medicinal springs of Malia.
My sad eyes were dimmed by nonstop weeping
    and the tears were a flood on my cheeks.
And the light through the weeping was like that from a spring
    that leaps from the mossy stones of a mountain peak
and is born headlong and hurtling down the valley
    till it crosses a road busy with people
and gives relief to the tired sweating traveller
    though the heat has cracked fields that were dry already.

There again Allius's help to me is like when sailors feel
  a gentle breeze in the right direction
just as the edge of the whirlpool gapes.
  He opened a path across his private land.
He gave my love and me his home
  so our affection could have fruition.
Bright with the light of a goddess my love entered
  on the worn threshold walking with ease on shining soles,
And her sandals clicked to her stately walk.
  Laodamia was hot with love for her spouse
when she arrived at the house of Protesilaus.
  They built that house in vain: no blood, no sacrifice
pacified the host of High Heaven. Nemesis
  let me not like anything so much
that I do it against the will of Heaven.
  When Laodamia had lost her man
she knew how much that altar had desired the blood it was owed.
  She had to let go her love's embrace
while the feel of it was still fresh
  before a succession of winters had satisfied her flesh.
She permitted it because the Fates foretold
  he would not be gone long
if he went as a soldier under Troy's walls.
  For that was the time of the abduction of Helen
when Troy brought down on herself the strong men of Greece.
  Troy – common grave to the known World!
Troy – man and virtue's bitterest ash
  that brought down Death on my poor brother.
My poor brother, snatched away, and all youth's light.
  With you is the death of this family.
The glory of our people passed away with you
  just as in life your affection made my days sweet.
You lie so far away – not among the tombs of your kin
  or the ashes of your fathers.
Your tomb is at Troy, obscene Troy that gods deserted
  – in a distant soil and an alien ground.

The young men of Greece were so quick they tell us
    to leave hearthfire and home.
They did not want Paris to add to the glory of his seduction
    and enjoy the carnal skills of his adulteress.
And that was your luck, Laodamia. In the spring of your need
    your life and spirit were taken away.
The passion that at its height had gathered you into itself
    hurled you down in an abyss
such as the one the old authors mention under a hill in Arcadia.
    It drained away the moisture from the marsh and left dry soil.
Heracles sucked out that mountain's marrow
    at the time he thought that his Father was mortal
and slaughtered the Stymphalian birds
    at the command of a lesser man.
He wanted to make a path for more gods to enter Heaven
    and Hebe to open her thighs for him.
But the height of your love was greater than the depth of your
                                                    [descent.
    What had brought you to marriage made you unbreakable.
Your love exceeded that of a Father who has grown grey
                                                    [and weary
    when his only daughter at last produces a grandson
and there is an heir to the estate
    and everything written down in due form
and the greedy faces of the next of kin
    no longer hang like vultures .
There was never a turtle dove that sang like that for her mate
    who is snow white too and rather more virile.
Doves in love never stop kissing I am told
    and show less inhibition than the female of the human.
But you Laodamia surpassed all lovers ever
    when you lay down with your corn haired groom.
The light of my life yielded little in quality
    as she came hurtling into my embrace.
And as she came I thought I saw
    Cupid in saffron glinting here and there.

117

I know that Catullus is just one man of many to her
    but I will bear with her promiscuities
and I will not trouble her with any jealousy.
    Juno is the greatest goddess in Heaven
and she knows that Jove is frequently unfaithful
    but she swallows her anger at his affairs.
Yet between Gods and Man there is no true comparison
    and we that are mortal have parents to bear with.
She did not come to me upon her Father's arm
    to a house made fragrant for marriage
but the signs she made me were secret
    and given from her husband's arms.
It is enough if she allowed me the one day
    that her white chalk scrawled on her calendar.
I created this, it was all I could do, Allius, for you.
    It is my gift of song. It is my thanks for many kindnesses.
I wish to stop your name being obscured by decay
    in the due succession of time.
And let the Gods add to my gift as much as she of Justice
    allowed to the righteous of time-past.
I want you to be happy, and the woman that breathes life into you
    in the place where I and she knew love.
And the same for him who made our world of love to form
    and was the beginning of the beauty that has ensued.
And let her be contented, who is dear to me above all others.
    Her life is the honey of my living, and my light.

PROPERTIUS

I needed a break away from my love,
    and now I address the kingfisher sea.
The goddess will not look at my boat with delight:
    prayer falls flat on a lee shore.
Though you are worlds away your winds remain:
    what threats a breeze can utter.
Can there be relief from the coming of the storm?
    Are these sands my resting place?
You could turn the storm to a calm
    but there is darkness and shoals.
Can you ask for my life and not cry?
    Can you deny yourself human flesh?
Let no one remember his name who first dreamed up oar and sail
    to cross the autonomous ocean.
Easier surely to cope with Cynthia
    who is wild yet herself
than to sail by forest shores without any name
    and mimic the world-altering brood of Tyndareus.
If the fates made a memorial of my grief
    and a stone marked the end of our affair
Cynthia would give her bright tresses as offering
    and lay out sweet roses
and declaim my name over my corpse
    and cry to the Earth to lie easy.
But sweet ocean daughters of the true spartan line
    set my white sails to a gracious tune.
If your waves know where Love has got to
    free a fellow slave and take him home.

HORACE

TO POSTUMUS

The years slip through our fingers, Postumus,
and Piety cannot keep us from wrinkles

or age or Death that has no lord.
No use – a daily sacrifice.

Three hundred bulls would be no use.
Pluto does not recognize tears.

He has Titans imprisoned by water.
And we must cross that water

who are favored with life on earth :
King or poor, there is no choice.

Though we avoided the monster of war
and the waves of the Adriatic

and were careful of the winds of autumn
we will observe Cocytus drifting black and slow

and the infamous spawn of Danaus
and Sisyphus who was Aeolus' son

damned to unending labor.
Home – and wife – will have to be left

and no tree shall remain with you
except the cypress that you hate.

A better sort shall inherit your wine
and what a hundred keys protect

shall end up on the floor
wine high priests might have drunk.

IV SAMUEL JOHNSON AND BAUDELAIRE

Baudelaire was a Romantic who grew up on the Classics, and inherited many of their values. Samuel Johnson was a classicist, who in English was deeply impersonal, but some at least of whose Latin poetry is altogether more of himself, more romantic.

SAMUEL JOHNSON

BY THE WATER MILL AT LICHFIELD

Like liquid glass
    through green meadows
that river still flows

in which once
    I bathed
my boy's limbs

confusing my arms
    with wrong movements
till my father's

kind voice told me
    how to swim.
There were branches

in which to hide
    and a tree hung over
and made those waters secret

and brought shade
    to the day.
But now that ancient dark

has yielded
   to harsh axes
and the bare flesh

of the swimmer
   is visible
to distant eyes.

yet the stream still flows
   in its tireless way
and though it flowed under branches

still it goes
   through openness
and though the outer world

hangs close and age
   bears down pursue
your own courses dear friend.

TO SKYE

In the far parts of the sea
   clamorous with storm
and planted with rock how graciously

Skye of clouds you offer
   your green bosom
to me who am weary.

Care I think is in exile
   from these lands, and peace
the habitant of these places.

No angry words, no upset
   in this quiet, no thought
of ambush now.

But no growing fat
   in cave of crag,
no use to the mind's torture

to wander the hills in their wilderness
   or stand on the cliff edge
and count the waves of the sea.

Human virtue is not to itself sufficient.

  No one has the chance
to make himself a calm sufficient soul.

That is the huge high fallacy

  of the twittering Stoic sect.
My king on high, my God

you alone rule, have the

  arbitration of
the overpouring heart.

The floods of the mind at

  your direction rise,
and so again decline.

BAUDELAIRE

THE ALBATROSS

Often for fun
      crewmen catch albatrosses
great ones of the ocean
          that follow

casual companions
         of the voyage

as the ship glides over
          the deathly deep

No sooner are they laid
          on the planks
than the Kings of Blue Heaven
          are awkward
ashamed
     letting
their wings
      trail
like oars
      beside them

winged voyager
         gauche
despicable

lovely sky swimmer
         a graceless joke

and someone would put
                    a pipe in its beak
and someone hobbles
                    to mimic
the cripple
            who flew

and the Poet
            is like
this cloud prince
                    who delights in the storm
and mocks
            at the archer
but exiled to Earth
                    and derision
the size of his wings
                    snarls his walk

V TWO IDYLLS OF THEOCRITUS

Theocritus wrote in Sicily and Alexandria a couple of centuries before Christ. He wrote of country people in real country dialect. The nearest thing this century is perhaps the Scottish Lallans poets. These pieces are more realistic than some others, where classical gods enter in to the landscape. His country folk are however always real, and it is a little hard to blame him for the unreality of the later Pastoral tradition. The translations use something of the North Country dialects of my childhood. My verse is perhaps more faithful to the sense than the rhythm of these glorious poems, the original is somewhat more mellifluous.

IDYLL 10

MILO

You fed up piece of mud, why you so sorry for yourself?
Not able to make a straight furrow like you used to,
and way behind your neighbors, left behind
like a sheep that's got a thorn stuck in its foot.
You're just beginning your furrows now, and scarcely
[getting on with it.
What you going to be like in the afternoon?

BUKAIOS

Milo you unfeeling stone chip
have you never mowed late because you wanted someone
[not there?

MILO

Never. What's love for someone not there when there's
[work to be done?

BUKAIOS

Never happened to you, you were too weak to move
[because you were in love?

MILO

God forbid! You shouldn't let a dog taste haggis.

BUKAIOS

But Milo I have been in love eleven days.

MILO

Obvious you're on the wine. Me I have enough with vinegar.

BUKAIOS

And so the fields before my door go unhoed.

MILO

And which of the girls messed you about?

BUKAIOS

She who played the flute not so long since
to the reapers at Mr Horseman's.

MILO

God find out the sinner. You've got what you always wanted.
A grasshopper from the fields to play touch with you all night.

BUKAIOS

You're beginning to make fun of me. But Cash is not
the only blind god. There's Love too. Don't talk so big.

MILO

I don't talk big. Just sow your land
and sing about the girl. And the work
will go nicely. There was the time
you were our best tune maker.

BUKAIOS

Muses sing with me a slender maid.
Goddesses whatever you touch make lovely.

Bombyka has all graces, and they call her the Syrian.
What to them is dried up and burnt is the colour of honey.

And the violet is swart, and the hyacinth marked,
but when garlands are to be made they are first to be picked.

The goat follows the clover, and the wolf the goat.
The crane has gone after the plough, but I still remember it.

Would it were mine – the wealth they say Croesus knew --
and gold images of us both would be offered to Aphrodite.

And there'd be a flute for you of applewood or rose,
and we'd have new shoes on both our feet.

Bombyka my love the noise of your feet is forgotten
and your skirts on your ankles. I cannot express it.

MILO

Its gone and got forgotten what good songs that other
[shepherd made.
Fine form, good harmony, appropriate meter.
I've grown up and got a beard in vain.
I just wonder at Literses' utterance.

Demeter of fruit, Demeter of grain,
may the tilling of this land
yield fruit in plenty.

May the binders of sheaves do it right
and none passing call them men of soft wood
not worth a day's hire.

Put your cut corn to the north
or let the west gaze on it
and then it will fatten.

Those that thresh corn should avoid
the afternoon sleep, for bran comes off
the stalk easiest then.

A reaper should begin with the lark
and end when he sleeps, and take good care
to stay out of the heat.

Froggy's got a happy life my boys.
No worry about someone to pour him a drink.
He's got more than enough.

Now steward we know you're on the make.
So you boil your lentils right,
and make sure you put some cumin in.

Oh that's the right song for men at it in the sun.
But your stupid love shepherd
that's something to tell your Mummy
when she gets up in the morning!

IDYLL 14

AESCHINES
Big greeting to big man Thyonichos.

THYONICHOS
Same to you Aeschines.

AESCHINES
An awful long time!

THYONICHOS
Long time, but why so sad?

AESCHINES
I'm not doing ok at all Thyonichos.

THYONICHOS
So thin, and the moustache so big
And the lovelocks all gone dry.
Just like that visiting Pythagorean
– He was grey to look at and barefoot.
Said he was an Athenian. Seemed to me
He was wildly in love with brown flour.

AESCHINES
You're making fun of me. The lovely Cynisca
Scorns me. I will howl with the mad
– I'm just a hair's breadth away.

THYONICHOS
Always the same Aeschines – such quiet passion
And wanting everything you can't have.
What did she say to you, the bitch?

AESCHINES
Had Argeios with me and that Thessalian jockey
Apis and Kleunichos for a drink (that soldier)
Out in the country at my place. I'd killed

Two chickens and a sucking pig, and opened up
Some four year old wine to make a feast.
And there was truffle and shellfish laid out by the winebutt.
Such good drinking!
And as the thing got moving it was decided
That we should drink to everyone's heart's desire
In wine without water. But we each had to name names.
And so having made our toasts we drank, as had been decreed.
But she said nothing with me there. And how do you
                       [think I felt?
'Why no toast? You seen a wolf?' gibed someone
'As the wise say', and she ignited.You could have lit lamps
Easily. There's Wolf you see, Wolf – our
                 [next door neighbor Labes' boy –
Tall and upspringing , and considered pretty by most.
Anyway this was the illustrious chap for whose love
                    [she was melting.
And someone told me about this in confidence.
And I did not investigate in vain into that grown man.
By now the four of us were deep in our drinking
And the Larissan chap struck up 'The Wolf'
That Thessalian tune, with mischief in his heart.
And Cynisca cried more bitterly than a six year old girl
That wants to sit on her mummy's lap. Then I
– You know me Thyonichos – thumped her forehead
Once, twice. She grabbed up her skirts
And she was off, so quickly.
'Stupid me' I cried out ' Not good enough for you.
You've got a mate who's sweeter. Go to him.
Cherish your love. Your tears for him are big as apples!'
The swallow is quick to get back
To her kids under the roof-reeds
And give them the mouthful of life she's gone out and found.

Quicker from her soft cushions she went
Through the hall and the double doors
As her feet led. Must be what they mean by
'The bull has gone to the wood'.
Twenty days since. And then Eight. And then nine. And
Ten more. Today makes eleven. Add two. Two months
Since I was with them. And I have not shaved, even dry
Like a Thracian. I know. Wolf's got it all. For Wolf
There's a way in at night. And I am not spoken of
Or worth reckoning anymore than the men of Megara
In the place of unworthiness. And if I could cease to love
All things would slide into their proper order.
But now – as they say Thyonichus – the mouse has tasted pitch.
What remedy or solution for love there is
I do not know. Except that Simos
Who loved the copper smith's daughter
Sailed away and came back whole.
And he was my age. And I will pass there
Across the sea, neither the best nor the worst maybe
But a good average foot soldier.

THYONICHOS
Should help to travel in your state of mind, if you want to
Aeschines. And if it seems the right course for you to go off
Well Ptolemy is the best paymaster for a man
                              [without commitments.
He's got a kind heart – loves the Arts – and he's a great lover –
And nice when it matters. Knows who's on his side,
                              [and – better still–
Who's not. Gives a lot of gifts to a lot of people. Refuses
Nothing asked a king should give. But don't ask for everything
Aeschines. And if it be resolved to pin up your cloak
On your right shoulder, and firm-set on both feet

To brave the onset and withstand the bold foe
Quick to Egypt! From the time of our birth
We grow grey, and by degrees on the chin
The white of time creeps. Do it if you must
                            [while your knees can bend.

Note: "Truffles" is strictly inaccurate. What is referred to is a small delicacy, still found in the Greek countryside, but with no English equivalent. Similarly we are not to imagine some large middle class place in the country, but a small cottage belonging to a town dweller.